Over **50** Killer Ideas
for Delivering Successful Projects

"Over 50 ways to help ensure project success"

By Richard Morrale

Over *50* Killer Ideas
for Delivering Successful Projects

2nd Edition

Multi-Media Publications Inc.

Oshawa, Ontario

Over 50 Killer Ideas for Delivering Successful Projects
by Richard Morreale

Acquisitions Editor:	Kevin Aguanno
Copy Editing:	Josette Coppola
Typesetting:	Peggy LeTrent
Cover Design:	Troy O'Brien
Incidental Graphics:	Rico Gusman, The JRL Partnership

Published by:
Multi-Media Publications Inc.
Box 58043, Rosslynn RPO
Oshawa, ON, Canada, L1J 8L6

http://www.mmpubs.com/

Published in Canada. Printed simultaneously in England and the U.S.A.

Paperback	ISBN-10: 1-897326-75-0	ISBN-13: 9781897326756
Adobe PDF ebook	ISBN-10: 1-897326-24-6	ISBN-13: 9781897326244
Microsoft LIT ebook	ISBN-10: 1-897326-26-2	ISBN-13: 9781897326268
Mobipocket PRC ebook	ISBN-10: 1-897326-25-4	ISBN-13: 9781897326251
Palm PDB ebook	ISBN-10: 1-897326-27-0	ISBN-13: 9781897326275

This book is dedicated to...

My sweetheart Linda and children Julie, Steve, David, Betsy, Susie, Matthew, Simon and Top Dog - Jake.

Acknowledgements

In terms of actually sitting down and writing this book, I'd like to thank the National Speakers Association for the 2004 convention where I was truly inspired to step up to the next level in my speaking career; to a number of speakers and authors who over the years, by their audio programmes, videos,seminars and books, have inspired me to get to the place where I am in my life. Special thanks go to Zig Ziglar, Jim Rohn, Les Brown, Anthony Robbins, Larry Winget, Mark Sanborn, Tom Antion, Dr. Wayne Dyer, my friend and fellow speaker, Larry Colbert and Tony Allesandra.

In terms of the content in this book, I'd like to thank the excellent Project Managers that I have worked for and the fantastic people that have worked with me on some of the most highly visible projects of the last 4 decades. Special thanks go to Joe Fischer, Bill Hopkins, Steve Matheson, Andrew Pinder and others far too numerous to mention here.

Contents

Contents *(cont.)*

Introduction

In the 1970s, surveys of major projects found that over 90% of them failed when measured against the criteria of cost, schedule and expectations. Most projects, if and when they were completed, either cost more than they were supposed to or took longer to deliver than they were supposed to or, if and when they were delivered, did not meet the expectations of the client.

So what did companies do? Over the next 30 years or so, they spent millions, if not billions, of dollars on project management "hard skills" training including planning, organizing, monitoring and controlling. In addition, they spent loads of money and development time on structured methods, tools and techniques to help them do their planning, organizing, monitoring and controlling. In no particular order, things such as work breakdown structures, product breakdown structures, configuration management, structured systems analysis and design method, structured development method, other analysis and development tools, Microsoft Project, PERT, Artemis, Project Managers Workbench, dependency networks, cost/ schedule reporting, and on and on and on...

So, after 20 years of spending a fortune on hard skills training, development and purchasing of methods, tools and techniques, there had to be a vast improvement.

In the 1990s, surveys of major projects found that... over 90% of them failed when measured against the criteria of cost, schedule and expectations. Should that not have made most intelligent people think that maybe hard skills were not where the problem was? Some people started catching on. However, not enough of them did because surveys early in the new millennium found that around 90% of projects were still failing when measured against the cost, schedule and expectations criteria.

So what is the answer? The answer is quite simple, really.

Delivery of successful projects is about 20% "hard skills" and about 80% "soft skills".

It is important for a Project Manager to have abilities around the hard skills as part of the success equation but overwhelming success depends on the soft skills such as enthusiasm, energy, commitment to excellence, commitment to success, going the extra mile, empathy, ability to motivate, communication, belief and a sense of humour.

I have had the opportunity to work with some really good Project Managers and some really good project team members who have worked on my projects and programmes. I have had the wonderful experience of learning a lot from both groups. The Killer Ideas in this book come from those experiences. In no way am I saying that these Killer Ideas are the only things you need to know to manage projects successfully. What I am saying, though, is that if you put some of these Killer Ideas into practice, your job as a Project Manager will be much more rewarding and you will have a much greater chance of success.

The Killer Ideas are in no particular order nor are they prioritized in any way. Just try them and let me know how you get on.

God bless you and happy managing,

Richard

Killer Idea 1
Foster a team atmosphere on your project.

I want the people working on any project that I'm managing to feel like they are part of a team. I know that when a group of people are working together as a team they are much more productive, they have more fun and they will deliver quality projects faster. How do you establish your project organization as a team? Well, there are a number of characteristics that must be met in order for the team concept to work. These characteristics include:

- Common purpose – the team must have a common purpose and they must all understand what that purpose is. As the Project Manager, it is your responsibility to ensure that the common purpose is communicated in such a way as to be understood by all.

- Goals and objectives – the goals and objectives for the team must not only be known and agreed by the team members. The Project Manager must ensure also by words and deeds that team members share responsibility for the achievement of the goals and objectives.

- Understand how each member of the team fits in – you must ensure that each of the team members understands the roles and responsibilities of both themselves and other members of the team and must understand what each of them are expected to do to deliver success.

- Achievement – achievement of the goals and objectives must be measured and made visible so that team members will know exactly where the team stands in terms of progress towards achievement.

- Ground rules – the team needs to establish the ground rules that define how the team will work together. These rules should also include how any conflicts will be handled.

- Success – the Project Manager should ensure that success is celebrated by the whole team and the whole team is recognized as responsible for the success, some members in an active role and some in a supporting role.

- Supportive environment – the Project Manager must ensure that the team operates in a supportive environment. Team members should be able to be open and honest without being concerned that they will be punished for their openness and honesty.

I took over a project once that had spent about 70% of its budget and had delivered about 30% of its products. And those were delivered to questionable quality. The company was seriously considering canceling the project. The project staff were really demoralized and couldn't see how they could succeed. After introducing the team concept into the project, being open and honest with them about the situation and asking for their help and ideas, they approached the project with a renewed vigor and were able to agree and deliver to an approved rescue plan. Sure, we were a little late in delivering to the initial plan. But we were right on schedule delivering to the rescue plan. We were over the original budget but within the budget established as part of the rescue plan. And the quality of the delivered product was second to none. I attribute this turnaround to the introduction of the team concept (and a great Project Manager, of course).

Obviously the above objectives are not the only ones that must be met for a team to be successful. But once these objectives are met, they go a long way to helping the team get established and operational.

"What you do on your journey
to delivering successful projects
is important – but more
important is how you do it."

Killer Idea 2
Lighten up.

There are certain characteristics that I believe a person should have to be a truly great Project Manager. Certainly, a Project Manager must have the hard skills associated with planning, organizing, monitoring and controlling the project. In addition, however, the Project Manager should also have soft skills that include, but aren't necessarily limited to, enthusiasm, energy, commitment to excellence and success, self-motivation, the ability to motivate the team, great interpersonal skills, excellent communication skills, honesty, openness and a really good sense of humour. That's right a really good sense of humour.

I was leading a seminar once with attendees from all over the world and by the time I listed these characteristics along with a few others on the flip chart one of the attendees, a beautiful lady from Italy, said, "If you find a man like that I'll marry him." I replied that if I found a man like that I'd marry him, although my wife and children would probably have something to say about it.

At any rate, I believe it is your responsibility as the Project Manager to establish an environment where team members can laugh and enjoy themselves. You must not take yourself too seriously. If someone is going to be the butt of a joke, make it you.

What we are delivering to the client is important and very serious and we should recognize that, but I also know that with a light atmosphere in place on the project, we have a much better chance of delivering the project successfully.

So, lighten up, enjoy yourself, make sure the team members are enjoying themselves and never, that's right, never take yourself too seriously. Have a great time!

"The average person working
8 hours a day for 40 years
spends about 70,000 hours at
work. That is too long a period
not to be having fun."

3

Killer Idea 3
Establish a project lending library of project management leadership and personal development books, audio tapes, videos compact discs and DVDs.

One of the best, long-term value-added actions you can take for your team is to establish a project lending library and help to foster an interest in management, leadership and personal improvement. I'm not talking about a library for filing the documentation developed during the project. That type of library is required and I will discuss it later.

What I am talking about here is a library containing books, audio tapes, videos, compact discs and DVDs dedicated to helping the individual become a better manager, a leader and to improve personally. I'm talking about messages from some of the best speakers and authors in the modern world.

When I suggest to members of my team and to those who attend my speeches and seminars, specific books that they should read, some of them sometimes use an excuse that they are so busy they don't have time to read. In fact, one person who used to work with me seemed to be very proud that he had not read a book since he was in school about 25 years before. Some people! Well, with audio tapes and compact discs, all they have to do now is listen. They can do this at the same time they are doing other things like driving their car. Zig Ziglar, one of the world's greatest motivational speakers and a man that truly inspires me, suggests that you turn your car into Automobile University. Instead of listening to the news or music, listen to something that's going to help you become a better person.

Most truly successful people will tell you that one of the keys to their success is that they are constantly learning new things. They read, listen and look at things that provide them with new ideas and help them become better at what they do.

I believe in this Killer Idea so much that at my speeches and seminars I sometimes give away products from some of the speakers and authors that I recommend. People such as Napoleon Hill, Zig Ziglar, Dr Norman Vincent Peale, Jim Rohn, Stephen Covey, Jeffrey Gitomer, Dr Wayne Dyer, Mark Sanborn, Larry Winget and Keith Harrell. Once you start on this path, I know that you will find others that excite you and you will want to add them.

*"It's worse to be able to read
and waste the ability than
not to be able to read at all."*

Killer Idea 4
Start every project with a detailed definition of the project.

Too many times, I have seen projects go bad because there wasn't a common understanding at the beginning of a project as to what was supposed to be delivered. People assume, even on small projects, that everyone has a common understanding of the deliverable and too late, everyone realizes that they don't.

I suggest that a detailed project definition should be completed before or at least at the start of the project. In fact, ideally, this should be the initial definition used to brief the Project Manager as to what the project is all about. What usually happens though, is that the Project Manager will have to produce this as the first deliverable and will get it agreed by whoever is sponsoring the project. In addition, once this detailed project definition is written and agreed, it should be used as the foundation to everything that follows. As changes are required, this document should be reviewed to see what the impact of the change is to the project at the highest level.

The detailed project definition will help you to stay focused on what it is that you are supposed to be doing. It will keep you from getting side-tracked and will help, if managed properly, in controlling the problem of "scope creep". Scope creep is changing the project requirements without considering of the impact on schedule and budget.

If you are assigned to manage a project that does not have a detailed project definition, you should make it your first task to create one. Prepare the document and get it approved by the powers that be before you start work on the project itself.

The detailed project definition should include items such as the problem to be solved by the project, the project's mission and objectives, the indicative required end date, the project scope, the indicative project budget, resource requirements, team roles and responsibilities, estimated project start date and estimated project completion date.

*Clarity concerning what needs
to be delivered is essential
at the start of the project.
A slight misunderstanding at
the beginning can cause big
challenges later."*

Killer Idea 5
Know what you are supposed to deliver before you start work on delivering it.

One of the top 10 reasons that projects fail is that people start working on the project before they really know what it is that they have to deliver. Sounds crazy, doesn't it. But it's true. I have audited loads of projects that were going bad and this was the major cause – no agreed requirements document. With no agreed requirements document in life cycle of the project, all sorts of bad things happen. Things like scope creep, eventual chaos, slippage in schedules, overruns in terms of cost and, in most cases, a deliverable that does not meet the expectations of the client.

So what is the solution? Well, it's simple but not necessarily easy. Get an agreed requirements document in place before you start working to deliver something.

The detailed project definition document discussed in Killer Idea 4 is a good foundation for development of the requirements document, but it provides a definition at too high a level. As the Project Manager, you need to get more detail in place before you can start building the end-product.

Preparing the requirements document can be done in a number of ways. One way is to interview the client to find out exactly what is wanted, document it and go back to the client to get the client's approval. This method probably takes the longest in terms of project schedule.

Another way to define the requirement is to hold a workshop with the client. The goal of the workshop would be to deliver, at the end of the work-shop, a documented, agreed requirements document. This method probably takes the shortest time in terms of project schedule.

A third way is to hold a visioning session. A few years ago, one of my clients asked me for a teambuilding course for 50 or so of her telephone fulfillment operators. Although she was sure that our standard teambuilding course was the thing they really needed, I wasn't happy with presenting it to her team because I didn't think it would deliver the outcome she was looking for. So I set up a visioning session. I facilitated and she and a couple of her supervisors attended.

I asked them to think ahead to after the training. How would her people be different? When she walked into their open-plan office, what would she hear? What would she feel? What would be the vibes in the room? What would she see? How would people be acting towards each other? From the answers to these questions, we formulated a vision statement that became the basis of the requirements for our training of her people. It also turned out to be the basis for testing after the training, so that we could see whether or not we had delivered the required outcome. The course we delivered turned out to be a lot different from our standard teambuilding course. Would our client have been happy with our standard course? Well, maybe. Would it have done the trick for her? I don't think so.

Look, no matter what techniques you use to define and capture the needs, make sure you prepare a requirements document, make sure you get it agreed, and use it as the basis for what you deliver. Use it as the basis for testing the finished product. You'll save yourself so much time, effort and money in the future, if you implement just this one Killer Idea.

"It's always better to know where you are going before starting a journey or you may end up some place you don't want to be."

Killer Idea 6
Never start preparing documentation without defining, as much as you can, the content and format standard of the document.

The main reasons that I'm suggesting that this should be done are to save time, to save wasted effort and to ensure that you produce the best document possible.

I suggest that before you start producing a document, you define it in terms of content and format. In other words, you should identify the structure of the document in terms of the various chapters, sections, sub-sections etc. and what goes into each of these parts. Identify each of the titles and document the type of information that should be included in each of them. Once that is done, assign various members of the team to the various sections and get on with it!

I once reviewed a major project for a large financial institution in London. The Project Manager said that the project was in the requirements analysis stage and that they were going to produce a requirements specification at the end of the stage. Further review, however, showed that no one knew the content or format standard for the requirement specification. Nor was there a detailed plan in place for producing it. After all, if you don't know what something should contain and how it should look, how could you put a plan in place to produce it? The project team were working on defining the requirement but they really had no idea how they were going to integrate the products they were producing into the specification.

I took over the project as the new Project Manager. The first thing I did was work with the team to define and agree the content and format standards for the specification. We then put the agreed structure of the specification into the data dictionary. As we produced each section of the specification, we populated the specification in the data dictionary. This method actually produces the specification as you do the work. It does not require you to gather data and produce the document later as so many projects tend to do. We did not have to do any additional work to produce the specification except send it around the team for review and comments. Once the comments were incorporated, we were able to baseline the specification and put it under change control.

This saved the team so much time and effort and enabled us to put together a very good requirements specification. And it all started with something as simple as an agreed standard for the requirement specification.

"Think of better ways of doing things. Be creative. Watch out that you don't fall into the 'This is the way we do it around here' rut. Change the way you do things. See what happens."

Killer Idea 7
Present to and agree with a project board or a project steering committee, the detailed project definition, requirements document and other documentation, as appropriate.

Killer Idea 31, dealt with later in this book, covers establishing a project Board or a project steering committee. But, let's assume that you have established either a project Board or a project steering committee already. For clarity, let's just call it a project Board. The major responsibility of the project Board is to direct the project and to provide you with high-level support when you need it.

I suggest that you get your key documents – the detailed project definition document, the project requirements document, the top-level schedule, the budget and other high-level items and documents of your choosing all, reviewed and agreed by the project Board.

Agreement by members of the project Board provides a number of benefits to the project. It provides visibility of the project to senior management who are representatives on the project Board. It also helps to ensure their commitment and gives them some "skin in the game".

Once they have agreed a document, they also have a responsibility for reviewing and agreeing changes to that document. This helps to ensure that the project Board members are not only aware of any impacts on costs, schedules, budgets etc. caused by agreed changes to the project, but they also are responsible for recognizing and approving those changes. And, if they approve the changes, they must, logically, approve the impact. There should be no surprises in terms of schedule slips, budget overruns etc.

*"Clear visibility helps to ensure
that there are no surprises."*

8

Killer Idea 8
Publicise the project goals and objectives by producing materials such as a goals and objectives wall poster, a laminated goals and objectives bookmark, goals and objectives mouse mat, etc.

One of the habits that successful project managers practice is the habit of staying focused. Staying focused on delivery of the agreed goals and objectives is not only important for the Project Manager to practice. It is also important for the entire project team and the project Board. One way to help the team stay focused is to make sure that whatever you want them to stay focused on is visible.

So make the goals and objectives visible. Print them on posters. Put them on the walls of the office. Put them in the meeting room. Provide laminated handouts to everyone. Put them on coffee mugs, mouse pads, and bookmarks.

Develop a project logo that typifies the goals and objectives. Use the logo on project documentation, letters, email banners etc. You and your team need to come up with ideas of where to make the goals, objectives and logo visible. Develop a project motto that also typifies the goals and objectives. For instance, when I was the project director for the Year 2000 programme for one of the major banks in England, I asked the chief executive what was his most important priority in terms of IT. He told me that his most important priority was to "keep the show on the road". In other words, keep the systems running so that the business could continue to operate. He said his other most important priority (I'm sure you've had more than one most important priority before) was to deliver the Year 2000 programme. We had a good think about what he said and came up with the motto "Y2K – keeping the road under the show". OK guys, so it's a little wet. It grew on us and we eventually used it as part of our Y2K logo. Add a little fun to the project and have a contest to see who can come up with the best logo and motto. Buy a bottle of champagne for the winner. Dip into your own pocket if you don't have the budget on the project to do it. It is worth it. Maybe the winner will give you a sip.

"A publicly declared and
written goal has a way of
transforming a good intention
into a real goal,
a dream into a plan and a
plan into a reality. Write it
down and make it happen."

Killer Idea 9
Use the workshop approach any time you need to get inputs from a number of people on the same project.

What is the one thing that most projects lack? An abundance of time. Most projects have a very tight schedule and anything that can be done to save time should be done, as long as it doesn't compromise quality. One thing that can be done is to use the workshop approach when similar information is required from a number of people.

Here's an example of what I'm talking about and how it saved loads of time on one of my projects. I took over a project for a large insurance company that had a plan in place and the team were just about to start on the requirements analysis stage. The output from that stage was going to be a requirements document. The plan showed 3 months for this effort. They were planning on conducting interviews with the client, preparing and presenting draft data flow diagrams to the client, incorporating client comments and presenting final data flow diagrams to the client for agreement. At the end of all of the interviews, drafts, comments and final agreement, the requirements document would be produced. As usual, we were under time pressure for delivery of this project for the client so we had to cut time but not quality wherever we could and this 3-month activity was a prime candidate.

We set up a series of workshops at the local hotel, where we were able to do the analysis in real-time. With the client present, we prepared the final data flow diagrams overnight and agreed them the next day. As the data flow diagrams were agreed, they were included in an already prepared requirementsdocument structure. We were able to cut the scheduled time for the analysis stage from 3 months to 3 weeks, knocking over 2 months off the schedule. Obviously we had to get the co-operation of the client, provide overnight support for preparation of the data flow diagrams and manage it closely to make it work. But it worked and saved us loads of time.

"Always be on the lookout for
ways of saving time while
maintaining quality."

Killer Idea 10
Produce and agree a document describing the project's detailed requirements.

T he first document in the project itself, after the detailed project definition, the overall project plan and other high-level documents, is the requirements document. In fact, the requirements document should be produced by the client and presented to the project team. However, this is very seldom done and therefore, most of the time, the project team becomes responsible for working with the client to produce the requirements document at the beginning of the project.

This document is absolutely essential to ensure success of your project. Without an agreed requirements document, you won't know what the client really wants. You might think you know, and in fact, the client might think you know, but I guarantee you this, on any project of any size, you won't know.

Without the requirements document, you won't know what it is you are supposed to deliver, you won't be able to put an accurate delivery schedule in place, you won't be able to put proper work packages in place or define the activities that must take place to deliver what the client really wants. In addition, you won't be able to accurately identify the cost of the project. Without the requirements specification, you won't be able to design what the client really wants, because you won't know what it is. You won't be able to test what the client wants, because you won't know what to test.

It is also important that you use some sort of structured approach to the production of the requirements document. There are loads of techniques available, so choose one and follow it. Most techniques work and most of the time when they don't work, the process is blamed when, in fact, the problem is the people. So stick with the process you adopt and fix the people issues.

Once the requirements document is completed, it should be signed by both the client and the project team. The client signs to signify that the document defines the requirements to be met by the project, and the project team signs to signify that they understand the requirements to be met. Also, I would have the project Board sign the document signifying their approval of the document.

Once agreed, any changes required to be made to the specification will need to be assessed in terms of technical impact, along with the impact on the project cost and schedule. If the proposed change is approved, then it follows that the impact to the project must also be accepted. That clarity saves a lot of arguments later.

"Just as it's important to know not only the country you are going to on holiday but also the details of where you are staying, it's necessary not only to know what you are delivering at a project level but also to know the details of what you are delivering."

Killer Idea 11

Identify and track unknowns.

This Killer Idea comes into its own, in most cases, during the preparation of the requirements document. As we work with the client in producing the document, one of the comments that the client and others raise is that they don't know the answers to some of the questions that we need answered to produce the document.

I believe that in most cases the information is either really known by someone in the client's organization, or it would not take much work to get it. So what should you do? Well, you should push as much as you can to get every question you ask, answered. Having said that, you need to understand that some things really are not known at the beginning of the project. In these cases, you need to make sure that you establish a data base to manage unknowns.

The data base should include at least the following for each unknown:

- Title of the unknown
- Description of the unknown
- When the information will be known
- Who is responsible for providing the information
- The risk associated with not knowing the unknown
- Mitigation action to be taken
- Comments.

This is a way to recognize unknowns and still ensure that they will, at some point, become known. In addition, it is a way of mitigating the risk associated with the unknown.

*"Knowing what we don't know
and tracking it is the only way to
ensure that eventually we know
what we don't know.
Understand?"*

Killer Idea 12
Identify the criteria to be used to accept that each of the requirements in the requirements document has been met.

This is accomplished by ensuring that each detailed requirement in the requirements section of the requirements document, has corresponding acceptance criteria in the acceptance criteria section of that document.

There are a number of benefits relating to the technical aspects of the project, by including the acceptance criteria in the requirements document.

The first benefit is in identifying holes that might exist in the detailed requirements. And we all know that errors found this early in the life cycle of a project are much cheaper to correct than if they are found later in the life cycle – say, during testing or, in fact, much later during implementation.

The second benefit is that once the acceptance criteria are identified and included in the requirements document, the design process becomes much easier.

The third benefit is in the area of testing. I like to set up an independent test function on my projects. We ensure that the requirements document is distributed to the independent test function so that they can test what the product is supposed to do rather than what the product does. Hopefully, this is one and the same. Clear acceptance criteria help the independent test team to prepare their test plans, procedures and scripts.

*"The benefits of knowing the
project acceptance criteria early
in the project far outweigh
the effort and cost of
identifying them."*

Killer Idea 13

Project planning is one of the most essential steps to take in the management of your project. Produce a good plan and go for it!

Before I get into the specific Killer Ideas concerning planning and how I recommend that you do it, there are a number of things that I would like to say about the subject at an overview level.

First of all, when I talk about a plan, I mean a scheduled list of interrelated stages, products, activities, milestones, tasks etc. along with assigned resources, estimated effort and planned elapsed time.

I believe that having a proper project plan is probably the second most important tool that the Project Manager must have. You probably can guess from my previous Killer Ideas what I consider to be the most important, even if just by a whisker, and that is the requirements document.

I'm a firm believer in what Zig Ziglar says and he was probably not the first one to say it. "Failing to plan is planning to fail."

Without an agreed, integrated project plan in place, how does anyone on the project have any idea what they are supposed to be doing, when they are supposed to be doing it, who is depending on them doing it, when the various milestones are going to be met, when the project will be delivered, and I'm sure I could think of loads of other things you wouldn't be able to do if I took the time. But I think you get the picture.

If you want to ensure project failure, discontent on the project and chaos, just don't put a good project plan in place. By the way, lack of a detailed project plan on a project is one of the top 10 reasons that projects fail. Want to know what the other 9 are? You can get a free e-book that I have written entitled, 'The Top 10 Reasons Why Projects Fail and What To Do About Them'by just going to my website www.RichardMorreale. com and subscribing to The Morreale Monthly, my monthly management, leadership and personal development newsletter.

In the introduction to this book, I talked about the project success equation being about 20% hard skills and 80% soft skills. Well, planning is absolutely part of the 20% that is essential for project success. The way in which you work with your team in putting it together, however, is part of the 80%.

So follow the Killer Ideas, produce a good plan and go for it.

"Give me a requirement and a detailed plan and I'm well on my way to success."

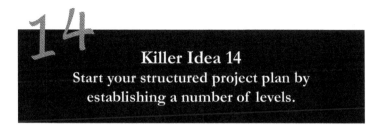

Killer Idea 14
Start your structured project plan by
establishing a number of levels.

The plan should be structured into a number of levels as shown in the following example diagram.

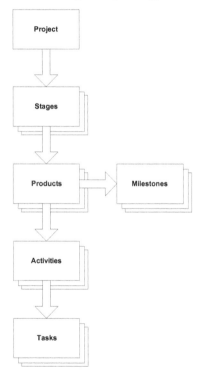

In terms of the plan, the project itself is the top level and successful completion of it can be broken down into a number of sequential, or slightly overlapping stages. Each stage can be broken down into at least one but, in almost all cases, a number of products. Each product is produced and delivered by completing a number of activities. Some project plans even break the activities down into tasks to provide greater granularity of the work required to produce the product. Milestones can be identified at whichever level you wish for tracking purposes. In terms of this example, I've established the milestones at the product level.

By the way, I don't care what names you give to the various planning levels, just as long as your planning is structured into logical levels. Some people might substitute the term phases for stages, deliverables for products, tasks for activities, and activities for tasks. It doesn't matter what you call the different levels as long as you pick one naming standard and stick with it. It's not the name that's important. The important thing is that you choose one.

However, for the purpose of clarity in this book, we will use the terms projects, stages, products, activities, tasks and milestones.

"A standard planning structure is key to producing an effective project plan."

Killer Idea 15
Adopt and introduce the project team to a 9-step planning process for planning the project.

The project plan on any of the projects I've managed, say over the last 20 years, was developed by following this 9-step planning process.

Each of the following steps is described in Killer Ideas 16 through 24 below. The steps are as follows:

- Step 1. Break the project down into major stages of work.

- Step 2. Identify the products to be produced and delivered in each stage.

- Step 3. Describe in detail the content standards of each of the products.

- Step 4. Produce an activity breakdown of the work required to produce each product.

- Step 5. Organize the activities into a dependency network.

- Step 6. Identify planning and estimating criteria for each activity.

- Step 7. Assign resources to each activity.

- Step 8. Schedule each of the activities either manually or by using an automated planning tool.

- Step 9. Smooth resources, as required, to create the optimum schedule.

This process will help you put a well-structured, comprehensive, realistic and achievable project plan in place.

The 9-Step planning process

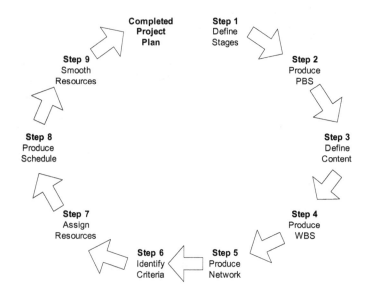

16

Killer Idea 16
Step 1. Start your planning with a breakdown of the project into major stages of work, with each stage delivering a major end-of-stage product.

A lmost every project can be broken down into major stages of work. In fact, I haven't found one yet that can't. Let's look at a couple of examples.

A project to build a house, for instance, could be broken down into stages and major end-of-stage products as follows:

Stage	End-of-stage product
Requirements Definition	Statement of requirements
Design	House plans/drawings
Build	Completed house
Acceptance	Owner inspected/accepted house

Each of these stages meets the requirements for a stage, in that they include major effort and the output for each stage is a major Product.

Similarly a project to build an IT system, could also be broken down into stages and major end-of-stage products as follows:

Stage	End-of-Stage Products
Project Initiation	Approved project initiation report
Feasibility Study	Approved system options/selected option
Requirements Analysis	Requirements document
Top-Level Design	Top-level design specification
Detailed Design	Detailed design specifications
Development	Developed system (code)
Testing	Tested system (code)
Acceptance	Client accepted system
Implementation	Implemented system

Any significant project can be broken down in the same way. This stage by stage and product-by-product breakdown is important because it forms the foundation of the project plan. It forces you, from the beginning, to think logically about your project plan and, eventually, everything that must be done to successfully deliver the project.

When done properly, it helps to ensure that nothing is missed.

17

Killer Idea 17
Step 2. Identify the products to be produced and delivered during and at the end of each stage.

I suggest that one of the last activities you perform in any stage is to put the plan together for at least the next two stages. As part of the 9-step planning process, step 2 says that you must identify the products to be developed and delivered during the completion and at the end of each stage. Therefore, if you are going to plan the next two stages you will need to identify the products for the next two stages as part of the whole process.

In my planning, I use a very loose definition of the term products. For instance, products can be management, technical or quality items. Let me give you a number of examples of each. Management products could be project management plans, weekly achievement reports, monthly achievement meetings, risk and issue reports etc. Technical products could be specifications, drawings, seating plans, design reviews, technical design meetings etc. Quality products could be quality management plans, quality reviews, quality review meetings, quality reports etc.

For instance, let's say that you were building an IT system in accordance with the example given in Killer Idea 16 and you were just finishing the requirements analysis stage. You should put together the plan for the next two stages - the top-level design stage and the detailed design stage. To do this, you will need to identify the products to be developed and delivered during both of those stages. It's as simple as that.

Each stage will have at least one product while so me stages will have more than one. In fact, in order to provide you with greater monitoring and control, I suggest that any product that will take more than 20 days to prepare, not counting review, re-work and sign-off, should be broken down into smaller products that can be integrated later to form the bigger product.

Without hard delivery checkpoints so that you can actually verify progress, you are completely at the mercy of the person preparing the products to report on progress. You've probably all heard of the "90% complete" progress statement. You ask someone on your project how close they are to completion and they say 90%. Then it takes almost as much time to do the other 10% as it did to do the 90%. Not very good. Make sure you have hard delivery checkpoints so that you know when it really is 90%.

"Identifying the products in each stage is all part of knowing what you have to deliver before you start working on delivering it."

Killer Idea 18
Step 3. Describe, in as much detail as possible, the content and format standards for each of the products.

Remember Killer Idea 5. It said, "Know what you are supposed to deliver before you start work on delivering it." Well, in Killer Idea 5, I was talking about the entire system or project that we were required to deliver. But the principle of that idea is the same, whether it is an entire system or an interim product. If you know what you have to deliver in terms of what the product will look like before you start, you will have a much better chance of defining and organizing the work to deliver it.

So, this idea is to sit down with a number of the people on your project team, take each of the products that you identified in step 2 and describe and document the content and structure for each of them.

For instance, as an example, a requirements document could be broken down as follows:

Section	Title	Description
1	Introduction	An introduction to the requirements document to include purpose, scope, background, controlling changes, etc.
2	Existing situation	A description in words, graphics, charts, etc. of the existing situation, system, etc.

3	Requirements	
3.1	Requirements introduction	An introduction to the requirements section of the document. An explanation of how each of the requirements will be represented, etc.
3.2	Detailed functional requirements	An introduction to the detailed functional requirements.
3.2.1	Requirement 1	Description of the requirement, as agreed, using graphics, diagrams, etc.
3.2.1+n	Requirement 1+n	Description of the requirement, as agreed, using graphics, diagrams, etc.
4	Constraints	Description of any constraints on the Project Team in the successful delivery of the Project.
5	Acceptance Criteria	Introduction to the acceptance criteria section of the specification. An explanation of how the acceptance criteria will be represented, etc.
5.1	Detailed Acceptance criteria	An introduction to the detailed acceptance criteria.
5.1.1	Requirement 1 detailed acceptance criteria	The acceptance criteria for requirement 1.
5.1+n	Requirement 1+n	The acceptance criteria for requirement 1+N

The above is only an example and not meant to accurately identify any specific requirements document standard for any specific type of system or project.

19

Killer Idea 19
Step 4. Develop and activity breakdown of the work requirement to produce each product.

Now that you have the project stages identified, the products for the next two stages defined along with a description of their contents, it is time to identify the activities that will be required to develop and deliver the products. Until you know the activities that have to be accomplished to develop and deliver the products, you won't be able to identify the process you will want the team to follow. You won't be able to estimate the time required to complete the product. And you won't be able to produce a detailed schedule for completion. That is why it is so important in this step to identify all of the activities for producing each product. In 'official' project management terms, this is called a work breakdown structure.

My suggestion is that you strive to establish, as much as possible, a generic series of activities to produce the products. In most cases, I've used the following generic series of activities for every product:

- Prepare draft.
- Hand-over for review.
- Review and comment on draft.
- Re-work draft with appropriate comments.
- Agree final version.
- Baseline final version.

Let me show you how that would work in practice. Using the content breakdown from the previous planning step as an example, and planning your activities at the lowest level of the content breakdown, here are two examples:

Example:

Covering the introduction section of a product

- Prepare draft introduction.

- Hand-over introduction for review.

- Review and comment on draft introduction.

- Re-work draft introduction with appropriate comments.

- Agree final introduction.

- Baseline final introduction.

Example:

Covering the requirement 1 + n section of a product

- Prepare draft requirement 1 + n section.

- Hand-over requirement 1 + n section for review.

- Review and comment on draft requirement 1 + n section.

- Re-work draft Requirement 1 + n section, with appropriate comments.

- Agree final requirement 1+ n section.

- Baseline final requirement 1 + n section.

Using a set of generic activities helps to make planning easier, helps to make it easier for team members to remember and work with the plan, and helps to make it easier to track and report on achievement. Establishing a generic set of activities that can be used for most of your products and therefore for most of the plan is easier than it might sound. Try it. You will be amazed at how easy it is to do.

Killer Idea 20
Step 5. Organize the activities into a dependancy network.

Once you have the activities identified for each of the products in the plan, the next step is to Organize the activities into the order in which they have to be accomplished. In other words, which activities must be completed prior to which other activities? Which sections of the products must be completed prior to other sections of the products? Which products must be completed prior to other products?

Organizing the activities, sections and products into dependency order – in other words producing a dependency network – will show you the process that the project team needs to follow in order to complete the plan.

This dependency network, when completed in the following steps with planning criteria, time-scales, resources etc, will also show the entire team how the project will be completed, who is dependent on whom, what is dependent on what and basically how it all fits together. It supports the team concept in that any member of the team can see how any slippage or lack of delivery on his or her part, will affect other members of the team and the project.

Dependency networks are fairly easy to do as there are numerous software planning packages to help in actually drawing the network. The important key is actually identifying the dependencies. Using the dependency network with the generic activities helps to make managing the project much easier.

"A step-by-step process makes it so easy to produce and manage whatever it is that you are required to deliver."

Killer Idea 21
Step 6. Identify estimating criteria
for each activity.

A lot of people classify the job of estimating effort and time-scales as a finger-in-the-air process – what some people call an educated guess. Some people say it is impossible to estimate accurately because we don't have enough information. Some people attempt to estimate at too high a level. Some people agree to a delivery date or give senior management a delivery date, just to keep senior management happy. They reckon that as the project progresses, they will be able to point to all sorts of things that might be affecting or causing the committed date to slip. I've seen all of this before and I'm here to tell you that, at this point in the planning process, you have all the information you need to provide an accurate estimate for the stages that you are planning.

The way you do it, is to sit down with affected members of your team, break each activity down to tasks that will be required to complete the activity and then estimate the effort and time-scales relating to each task. Add those up and you now have the estimate for the activity. Add the estimates and time-scale up for all of the activities required to produce a product and you have the effort and time-scale for the product. Add the effort and time-scales up for all of the products in the stage and you have the estimate for the effort and the time-scales for the stage plan. OK, so it's not exactly that easy and, as the Project

Manager, you must continually challenge the estimates for any extra contingency being introduced by the team. But it's almost that easy to get accurate estimates of effort and timescales. Follow the process.

Remember, breaking the activity down to its various low-level tasks and then estimating the tasks provides you with a much more accurate estimate of effort than any other way of estimating.

"Maintaining a history file of planning vs actual information on past projects can help you plan similar projects now and in the future."

Killer Idea 22
Step 7. Assign resources, resource numbers and resource types to each activity.

Now that you know what must be delivered, the work to be accomplished in delivering it, the order in which the work must be done and the estimate for the amount of effort to do the work, it is time to assign resources to each activity and task. It is best at this point in the process to know the resources by name. However, if you don't know their names because they haven't been assigned to you yet, then you can identify the resources by job function.

There are a number of situations that you could now find yourself in. The first could be that you have been given a team of people to deliver this project. The second could be that you have been told to deliver by a certain date and you must identify how many and who you want on your team. The third situation could be that you have been given a certain date and the team you have to deliver with by that date. The fourth situation could be....... There are a whole bunch of possible situations left. At any rate, now is the time to identify the number, skills and type of team members you will need. I suggest that you not only identify the hard skills you want the individuals to have but also the soft skills, behaviors and attitudes.

If you have been given the people for your team and they are not right for you, or there are not enough of them, or some or all of them are unacceptable for whatever reason, or you have not been given any people at all now is the time to fight for them – the right people and the right number. Use the detailed project plan that you are developing as the back-up you need to prove your case.

"If I had a choice of a person with the right attitude but lacking some experience, or a person with loads of experience but a bad attitude, I'd take the first one every time."

Killer Idea 23
Step 8. Schedule each of the activities/tasks either automatically, using an automated planning tool, or by hand.

The schedule is simply produced as an outcome of the effort required on an activity, divided by the number of resources that can be and have been assigned to that activity. So it is not very difficult to work out a schedule either by hand or by using an automated planning tool such as Artemis or Microsoft Project.

When I first moved to the United Kingdom from Virginia, I was responsible for putting together the plan for the computerization of Britain's Pay-As-You-Earn (PAYE) income tax system. The entire plan comprised approximately 7700 activities for about 110 major products, with about 2200 of those activities on the critical path. The 2200 critical path activities were a generic set of about 20 activities for each of the major products. Those 2200 were the ones that had to be scheduled. The other 5000 or so had to fit in around the critical path activities.

I remember a weekend at my house in Shrewsbury, England, when I removed the pictures from the living room walls, put flipchart paper on the walls around the entire room, divided the flipchart paper into weekly increments, listed the 110 products down the left-hand side of the first page and started scheduling the project by hand, drawing the 20-activity, generic dependency network for each of the products. It took two of us the whole weekend to complete the schedule, because once we drew the initial schedule completing Step 8, we moved on to Step 9 of the planning process, which is described in the next Killer Idea.

"Producing an activity schedule is simple. The scheduling equation for any activity is EE/R = ET where EE is the estimated effort for the activity in man-days or man-hours, R is the amount of resources available in the same units as the estimated effort and ET is the elapsed time to complete the activity."

Killer Idea 24
Step 9. Smooth resources, as required, to create the optimum schedule.

Most automated planning systems advertise that they can be used to automatically smooth resources to the optimum use, thereby providing the best possible schedule. They say that they take into consideration the activities, effort estimate and resources that have been allocated, either by name or resource indicator, and the estimated elapsed time for each activity.

Well, I'll tell you what happens. They might do it totally logically, with the above information fed into the system, but they don't have much common sense built into the algorithm. So, what do you get? You get 7-day activities which should be started and logically continued until they are completed being broken up into three, 2-day activities and one 1-day activity and being completed over a much longer period, in terms of the schedule. The system will take a resource assigned to, say, 3 activities, get the resource started on the first activity, maybe complete 20% of it, move to the next activity, maybe complete 50% of it, move to the third activity, complete all of it, go back to... This is getting confusing! You know what I'm talking about.

I can hear some of you saying, well, the smoothing will work if you put in the accurate information about what can be broken up and what can't. Well, in my experience, you end up having to put so much information into the system that not only does the system bog down, but the dependencies get so complicated that it ends up in a great big mess.

My advice to you is to spend some time and do the smoothing as much as possible by hand. OK, some resources might be slightly over-utilized but that's what your job as a Project Manager is about. Work the situation. I believe that to ensure that you get the best use and spread of the resources that have been assigned or that will need to be assigned, the only way to do it is by hand. So call me old fashioned; it just works better

Once you have smoothed the resources, take the dates that you end up with for each of the activities, input those dates into your system and track achievement to them. It will be so much easier.

Take the time up front to work through all the steps of this 9-step planning process, and you're wind up with a plan that you... and your team... and the client... can rely on. And that'll let you sleep easier and manage better.

"I may be getting old but
sometimes I think it's easier
to do it manually instead
of with computers.
And that's it."

Killer Idea 25
Plan your projects down to activities with a maximum elapsed time of 5-10 days.

I break my projects down to activities with a maximum elapsed time of 5- 10 days. There are a number of good reasons for this.

First of all, in the planning stage, it is easier to estimate the total effort for the project and the elapsed time for an activity, if the activities are broken down to this 5-10 level.

In addition, it is easier to monitor achievement of 5-10 activities on a regular basis than it is to monitor activities that are scheduled to take a longer period of time. For instance, I think all projects should be monitored on a weekly basis so you will be able to keep close track of achievement. When you are monitoring on a weekly basis, if a 5-10 activity is going wrong, you know about it early and because of that you have the opportunity to do something to bring it back on track.

If you are monitoring a 30-day activity on a weekly basis you will need to depend on the person working on the activity to provide you with an estimated completion status. And, as you know, most people are fairly optimistic when they provide an update. So you can't be sure the update will be accurate. In addition, 30-day activities are usually not reported as slipping until close to the delivery date. Most of the time this does not give you time to take action to bring it back on track.

Some people feel that planning at the 5-10 level is taking the plan down to too low a level. If that bothers them, what I'm going to propose now will probably drive them crazy. Some of the activities that I monitor last less than a single day. Let me explain the criteria I use for planning in the next Killer Idea.

"Plans broken down to too low a level add a large monitoring and reporting overhead to the project; plans at too high a level do not give you the control you need to manage effectively."

Killer Idea 26
Use standard criteria for identifying activities that last 5-10 days.

I use a number of standard criteria to determine when I should establish a new activity. Let me explain.

If the elapsed time for completion of an activity is estimated to be more than 5-10 days, I find some way of breaking the activity down to a lower level of detail, so that the elapsed time is 5-10 days or less. For instance, say the activity is to produce a specification and it has been estimated that it will take approximately 30 days to produce it. Then for the purpose of getting the activities down to no more than 5-10 day levels, I will break the specification down into smaller deliverable chunks, such as chapters and this would probably do the trick. If it doesn't, I then work to break it down even further. The goal is to get to the 5-10 day level.

I also establish a new activity when the responsibility for the work to be achieved changes. For instance, if we continue with the production of the specification as an example, we find that the activity "produce the specification" actually is made up of 5 activities.

These five activities are:

- Produce the specification.

- Hand over to the review group.

- Review it and comment.

- Incorporate applicable comments.

- Issue the agreed specification.

Then suppose that the responsibility for achieving each of the activities changes. For planning and tracking purposes in addition to ensuring clarity about who is responsible at various times in the process, I break the activity "produce the specification" into it's five components in the plan. That way there's no doubt about who is responsible for each part.

"Time spent on putting together a well thought out, structured, accurate, detailed plan is well worth it and will pay back huge dividends as the project progresses."

Killer Idea 27
Ensure that all activities in the product plan, help to produce a deliverable product.

Considering that the total project is made up of deliverable products (see Killer Idea 17), all activities in the project plan must, help to produce a deliverable product. If an activity doesn't help to produce a deliverable product, then why are we wasting our time doing it? So if you end up with activities that are called dangling activities, meaning activities that are not linked into an existing deliverable product, you should ask yourself a number of questions.

Why is this particular activity being done? What is going to be the outcome of this activity? Are we going to get information that we require from completing this activity? What deliverable product requires this information? Have we missed a product in our planning? Have we missed linking this activity to a deliverable product? With the answers to these and other questions that you ask yourself, you should then either link this dangling activity to an existing product, add a new product or delete the activity. Don't leave it dangling.

"All activities must be linked to a deliverable product or they shouldn't be in the project plan."

Killer Idea 28
Involve the project team, as much as possible, in the planning process.

One of the worst things a project manager can do is draw up a plan, independent of his or her team, and then present it to the team as the gospel. When this happens, the team has no commitment to the estimates, activities, products, or anything else.

You must involve your team in the planning process as much as possible. If you don't have your team in place when the plan needs to be drawn up, then draw up the plan and make sure when new members join the team that you present the plan to them, get their input, modify the plan if required, and get their commitment to estimates of effort and time, to achieve the various parts of the plan. Their buy-in is essential if the plan is to work.

Some time ago, I was contracted by a large insurance company to head up a project that should have taken about 3 years to complete but they had been working on it for approximately 5 years and it still wasn't finished. The estimate for completion at that time was for another 2 years but no one trusted the estimate. In fact, as I found out later, the 2-year estimate was strictly a finger-in-the-air-guess. The project was to replace all of their existing IT systems. One of the first things I looked at was the existing plan, or should I say, the lack of an existing plan. The project had degenerated into six different teams working on a number of IT programmes, with each of the teams being managed by the seat of the manager's pants and with plans on the back of a cigarette pack. OK, that was a little exaggeration but it wasn't far from that. I felt that one of the first things that I should do was to put a good structured plan in place so that everyone knew what they were supposed to be doing, when they were supposed to be doing it and who was dependent on them doing it. I also knew that I couldn't just dictate a process and a plan to them. First of all, I didn't know enough about the project to do that and even if I did know enough and dictated a plan, they would not be committed to it. So I had to get them involved in dictating the process and reflecting the process in an agreed plan if we were going to put a good plan together.

The six project managers, my project support manager and I followed the planning process introduced in Killer Idea 15 and over a period of approximately 2-3 weeks, put a very good plan in place. During those 2-3 weeks, each of the project managers discussed the development process and the planning estimates and so on with their individual teams and got their commitment. As the programme manager, I challenged estimates and led the process and, at the end of the planning period, we had an excellent plan in place. The new plan covered a 13-month period that we basically stuck to for the rest of the project. The teams responded very well to the new process and programme of work and we delivered on time.

*"Sometimes you have to take a step
backwards to make forward progress."*

Killer Idea 29
Base all of your planson deliverable products.

It is essential that your project plans are based on deliverable products. It is easier to manage the production of a deliverable product than to manage a number of functional activities. Take, for example, analysis of the project's requirements.

During the analysis phase of a project, I could identify, in my plan, various activities that I think need to be completed to prepare things that I might eventually need to pull together into the requirements document. I could also then have an activity in the plan, at the end of the stage, to "produce a requirements document". There are a number of problems associated with this way of planning and completing the work. Most of the time, once all of the analysis is completed, the document doesn't get produced. People say they will produce it later but they never get around to it, and without it, they can't put the necessary scope-creep controls in place. Also, if the work is done independently of the production of the document, how can you be sure that you are doing work that needs to be done, or whether you're leaving out some things that do need to be done? You can't be sure.

When you base your plans on deliverable products, you know ahead of time what the delivered product is going to contain. So you know that you won't be doing any work that is not required. In addition, the document is prepared as the work is accomplished. Therefore, there is no need to wait until all of the work is done to start producing the document. You cut out the option of the team saying, we'll do the document later.

Build all of your plans around deliverable products and you will have a much better chance of success.

"A well structured, detailed project plan can be used for a number of things in addition to determining how long a project will take to deliver. It can also be used to:

- Gain commitment of the team, bosses, peers, business and users.

- Help to instill a teamwork culture in the project team.

- Get required resources.

- Identify how the required project delivery date can be met."

Killer Idea 30
If at all possible, ensure that the entire team is co-located.

If there is one thing I hate when I'm running a project, it is to have my project team spread out all over the place. I like to have all of my team sitting in the same place. I'm well aware that this is sometimes difficult but if at all possible you should do what it takes to make it happen.

Instilling soft skills into the team is much easier when the team members are in one place. It is easier for the team to be motivated, to be more passionate about the project, to be more committed to delivering a quality product, to be more helpful with each other, to share responsibility, and to celebrate success when they are located together.

It also provides a better environment for good communication within the team. I believe that poor communication is one of the ten main reasons for project failure, so, the better the communication, the better chance the project has to be successful.

By the way, I'm not just talking about the IT people. I'm also talking about the users that have been assigned to the project. Now I know that some of you are saying that that truly is impossible. Well, when I took over a major project at a large insurance company, I was able to convince the user senior management not only to assign a number of users to the project on a full-time basis, but also to assign a number of others to test the system on a part-time basis. In addition, when both the full-time and part-time user resources were working on the project, they shared the office with the project team. It really helped ensure that the final delivery of the product was on time, within budget and met the expectations of the users.

One of the other situations that project managers are running into these days is parts of the project team working at home. I find it very difficult to run a successful project with a large part of the team working at home. I don't mind someone working at home with a specific task or activity to complete as long as the work can be done independently of others. If I were you I would attempt to avoid homeworking as much as possible.

"I believe that managing a project without having the team co-located, especially if part of the team is working at home, is about as difficult as herding cats."

31

Killer Idea 31
Establish and use to your advantage, a
project Board or a project steering committee
comprising, at least, senior representatives of the
developers, the clients and the users.

There are going to be plenty of times during the project when you, the Project Manager, will have difficulties that you will not be able to overcome on your own and you will need help from senior managers. So, as a Project Manager, I feel it is important to have someone or some group I can turn to when I need help to get something done in the client's, the users, or the developer's organization.

For this reason I believe it is of utmost importance that the Project Manager establishes, specifically for his or her project, a project Board or a project steering committee, or whatever it is that you want to call it. The important thing is that you make sure, in whatever way you can, that you get the right people on to this group. As a minimum, I would have a senior representative from the developer's organization, a senior representative from the client's organization and a senior representative from the organization that is going to actually use what is being delivered. If the project sponsor is not one of these representatives, then make sure he or she is also in the group.

These representatives must be at a level enough that they can take decisions for their area of the organization. They must also be able to make things happen when you need things to happen. They need to be able to deliver. They must be truly committed to the project and to the project's successful delivery. These people need to know what they are doing. In a real sense they are directing the project, but at the same time they are servants to you and your team.

You need to remember this – a project Board appointed to just "tick-thebox" is worse than having no project Board at all. With a "tick-the-box" project Board we have the false impression that we've got help when we need it, only to find out too late that they do nothing for us. At least without a project Board, I now from the beginning that I am going to have to handle every challenge that the project faces.

Just do it. Put a project Board in place and reap the benefits!

"Helping to choose the right people for your project Board or, at the very least, influencing who is appointed to your project Board can put you in the driver's seat of your project's future."

32

Killer Idea 32
Make sure that you have a project sponsor, who is in a position of authority, will "die-in-a-ditch" for the project and can make things happen for you.

U sually the project sponsor is the person who holds the budget. And I've always believed in the Golden Rule. Some people believe that the Golden Rule is "Do unto others as you would have them do unto you." However, the Golden Rule that I'm talking about here is the one that says "The person with the gold makes the rules." So the person with the budget makes the rules and that person, the person spending his or her money, should be the project sponsor.

First of all, I want to make sure that the person who holds the budget really wants what I am being asked to deliver. If they don't really want it or if they are not committed to paying for its delivery, then I have to question why we are doing it. I must have this "die-in-a-ditch" sponsor. Believe me, if I don't have a truly committed project sponsor, I will go to senior management to ask for one. If they won't give me one then I have to decide whether I want to manage this project at all. Because, sure as the sun will come up tomorrow, there will be problems on my project that I will need to go to the sponsor about and I know that an uncommitted project sponsor is someone that I don't want to deal with.

Once I'm sure that the person holding the budget is also my project sponsor and I'm sure that my project sponsor is committed to my project succeeding, I then need to make sure that the project sponsor is on the project Board, where he or she can take an active role in the direction of the project.

Sometimes, I have had to fight the appointment of a project sponsor who was selected to be the project sponsor because he or she wasn't particularly busy. No good! You must be aware that this happens and if it does happen to you, fight it!

"It is essential for the project sponsor to be committed, active and supportive. Make sure you start your project off with a sponsor with these characteristics and keep yours on your side."

Killer Idea 33

Establish an Independent test team, or an individual on you project team, with the responsibility of ensuring, through the testing process, that what you are delivering meets the requirements of the client.

I know that you can't test-in quality but you sure can determine if what you are testing is quality. As I was working on projects and serving what I consider to be my apprenticeship in project management - more years ago than I care to remember – one of the things that kept happening was that testing always got squeezed at the end of the development process. Design of the product could slip, development of the product could slip but testing couldn't slip because senior management always wanted to meet the end date, if at all possible. In a lot of cases, senior management took the decision to squeeze testing and do less of it. I always felt that this was a sure-fire way of delivering a poor system. The attitude was "We'll just put it out there and fix the problems as they occur". The big issue with that, of course, is that, generally, the cost of fixing the delivered product or system is a lot higher than the cost of fixing the product or system before it's delivered – cost, measured in money and reputation. In fact, as we all know, the earlier an error is found in the development cycle, the cheaper it is to fix.

Another thing I noticed about testing was that the same people who designed and developed the product or system were, in most cases, used to test the product or system. The issue with that, I've found, is that the developers test the system for what it will do, not necessarily what it is supposed to do. Now those two things should be the same but in most cases they are not.

So what is the solution? Well, in the first situation, where everything on the project can slip but testing, the solution is to hope that we have a really good Project Manager who will make sure that testing is not squeezed.

The solution to the second situation is fairly simple. Establish an independent test team, or an individual on your project team with the responsibility of ensuring, through the testing process, that what you are delivering meets the requirements of the person that wants it. Ensure that they use the latest agreed version of the requirements as the basis upon which to write their test plans and scripts.

I've established an independent test team on every project that I have managed over the last 20 years. I would never run a project now or in the future without it. I'm sold on the idea and I hope you are.

"Never be pressured into
releasing a product or
system into implementation
if that product or system
has critical errors."

34

Killer Idea 34
Establish a project support office, resourced with people with the responsibility to make the project manager and the project team's jobs easier and more focused.

As we all know by now, the role of the Project Manager is to plan, Organize, monitor and control the project.

In addition, we have found that the hard skills associated with doing these four things are about 20% of what ensures project success. We know that the other 80% has to do with attitudes such as enthusiasm, energy, commitment to excellence, commitment to success, honesty, openness and sense of humour, and with behaviors such as spending time with the project team, wandering around, staying in touch, motivating people, spending time with clients, managing the client's expectations and going the extra mile.

We also know that, for projects to be successful, we must not only plan the project but must also document the plan, monitor achievement and maintain the plan on a timely basis. In addition, we must manage, control and report on changes; identify, manage and administer risks and issues; identify, manage and report on dependencies; establish and maintain a documentation library; manage the review process; manage and report on action items; prepare and distribute reports on project achievement; and prepare for and attend achievement meetings, project Board meetings, and the like.

If you leave all of this up to the Project Manager, I can guarantee you that it won't all get done. The urgent stuff of the moment will get done and the rest will be put aside to do later when the Project Manager gets a chance and most of the time that chance won't come.

Also, why should an expensive resource like the Project Manager doing things that can be delegated to a less expensive resource?

Remember, the Project Manager should be spending most of his or her time with the project team and not in his or her office. So what is the solution? Delegate it. Establish a project support office.

A project support office can be resourced by one person on a small project, or as many as 15 people on a project of, say, 200 people. When I was programme manager for a major High-Street bank in the UK with approximately 350 people in my programme, I had a project support office of approximately 20 people. A typical project support office budget should be 5-10% of the project budget in terms of staff.

A project support office is a very cost-effective way to provide help and assistance to the project manager and the project team in all of the project discipline areas that are required for project success. These areas include project planning and control, configuration management, including change control, quality assurance, documentation management, risk and issue management, and dependency management. How the project support office provides the support in each of these areas is covered in other Killer Ideas:

- Killer Idea 43: support in project planning and monitoring.

- Killer Idea 44: support in the achievement reporting process.

- Killer Idea 45: support in the change control process.

- Killer Idea 46: support in the set-up and operation of the project library and the document review and approval process.

- Killer Idea 47: support in the dependency management process.

- Killer Idea 48: support in the the project risk and issues management process.

35

Killer Idea 35
Remember the "3 Amigos."

I believe all projects should be managed by a team I call the "3 Amigos".

The first Amigo is the Project Manager, The second is the technical director and the third is the project support officer.

Although I have successfully managed some really huge technical projects in my life, I do not come from a technical background. As you can see from my personal bio at the back of this book I had lots of different jobs until I started working on the Apollo programme as a messenger, and my college degree is in Business. I'm not saying that I can't understand technical issues but I do not have the experience necessary to really dig into the technical aspects of some projects. And, by the way, I am not all that interested. I think that project managers should not get all that involved in the technical aspects of the project, anyway.

When I was assigned to manage my first project, I obviously took the job even though I didn't have a technical background and the project was a highly technical one. So what did I do? I worked out a plan that showed that I needed some hotshot technical people. They were assigned to me and I made one of them my technical director. Her name was Rebecca and she was just great. Her job was to spend all of her time on technical issues and brief me on the various options associated with them. My lack of technical experience didn't keep me from being smart enough to understand the issues. My job was to consider not only the technical issues but also the ramifications around cost and schedule, and make the decisions. It worked just great and it was on that project, early in my career, that I realized that by appointing a technical director, who understood the technical issues associated with the project, I could manage any project. I am not a civil engineer but I know that I can build a bridge or a building. A really good Project Manager, with a really good technical director, can take on almost, type of project and deliver it.

The third Amigo is the project support officer who either manages a project support office (if the project is big enough) or is the project support office (if the project is not big enough to have a project support office team). This person is responsible for supporting the Project Manager and the rest of the project team in the areas already discussed in Killer Idea 34.

I believe in the "3 Amigos" concept and I will never run a Project without my other two in place. And you should not consider doing it either.

"A Project Manager with confidence,
belief in himself and his project team,
an understanding of both the 20% hard
skills and the 80% soft skills, and the right
Amigos can deliver almost anything."

36

Killer Idea 36
Identify the skills, attitudes and behaviors you believe you need as a Project Manager and establish a personal development plan.

I have written a number of times in this book that I believe successful project management is about 20% hard skills as they relate to planning, organizing, monitoring and controlling – and about 80% soft skills as they relate to attitudes and behavior.

One of the important things that I believe Project Managers should do is to identify which attitudes and behaviors they believe they need to have to be a truly successful Project Manager. Some of the soft skills that have come up when I've asked my audiences to tell me what they believe is required are, in no particular order, enthusiasm, energy, honesty, professionalism, good communication, empathy, openness, approachability, sense of humour, fairness, passion, go-for-it approach, commitment to excellence, commitment to success, an extra miler, caring, and being a good listener and motivator. You may come up with different soft skills.

Whatever you come up with, identify the top eight characteristics that you feel you need have to be successful and grade yourself on a scale from 1 to 10 in relation to each of the eight characteristics: 1, so poor you almost get suicidal thinking about it; and 10, so good that people throw rose petals in front of you as you walk in the office. Don't spend too much time on analyzing where you are on the scale, just rate yourself by your gut feelings. Once you've done this, you will have a list of attitudes and behaviors that you (not someone who has told you, but you) believe you require to be a truly successful Project Manager and you'll know where you could devote some time to getting better.

I would use this information as the basis for my personal development plan. I suspect that you rated yourself somewhere between a 3 and an 8 on most, if not all, of your characteristics. So you could really improve in most areas. Search for those things that will help you get better in the areas where you need to get better. Start studying, reading, listening to audio tapes and CDs recorded by some of the truly great personal development speakers and authors. Practice what they recommend and then, every six months or so, go through the same exercise of rating yourself and see how you are doing, compared with your previous scores.

Suggest to your project team that they do this also.

I believe if you do this you will see yourself becoming more successful in dealing with people and in managing your projects.

"There are some really great books that you can
read to help you develop the 80% soft skills.
Go to my website at www.RichardMorreale.com
and check out my recommended books.
You don't have to buy them from my site but,
for your sake, buy them. Oh! Read them, also."

37

Killer Idea 37
Get signatures on hard copies of
all baseline documents.

The main reason that I want to get signatures of approval on a hard copy of a document, rather than getting an agreement by email, is because I use the time for getting the signature to help me to get commitment from the person signing. In addition, I want to make sure that the person signing the document has reviewed it and understands the responsibilities he or she is signing up to. By all means, use email to pass the document around for review and comment first. But when it comes down to getting it agreed, print a hard copy version and meet with those that must sign it, to get their signature. I have even had a meeting of all the signatories, where I presented the final copy of the document and then passed it around for signature. I've done this with business cases, requirements documents, project management plans, and many other key documents.

Once the document is signed, why not have a celebration. Pop open a bottle of mineral water or something a little stronger. When I was one of nine programme directors of a 3-year major change programme for one of the largest banks in London, we each had to get a business case approved once a year. Approval meant getting the signatures of approximately 15 senior managers. All of the programme directors and various support staff met once a week on a Thursday morning from

8:30 to 10:30. The day after I was the first successful programme director to get my business case approved, I showed up at the Thursday meeting, announced that we had been successful in getting the business case signed and proceeded to haul in a few bottles of champagne and orange juice and we celebrated the occasion, throughout the meeting, with a number of Bucks Fizzes. Judging by how well the meeting went, we all felt that it was something we should have done more often. Get hard copies of documents signed, get commitment, and celebrate.

"Most Project Managers hold a celebration once a project has been delivered. I don't think that is enough. Think of good reasons to celebrate throughout the project and keep the team spirit high."

Killer Idea 38
Ensure your client understands and agrees the amount of time they will have to spend on making the project a success.

One of the things I dislike is the client who wants what you are delivering to him or her, but constantly says that neither they nor their people have time to spend on making the project a success. It is imperative that they – the client and the client's people – must spend time on the project if you are going to deliver the project successfully.

You need them to help with the preparation of the requirements document. They should be responsible for the preparation of the acceptance test specification. They must be available for management and technical achievement to take the time necessary to prepare for and to attend the project Board meetings. They need to be available for review and comment on other project documentation. There are loads of things that the client must do to work with you.

One thing I have done in the past and require all of my project managers to do now, is to make sure that the required amount of client time is included in the project initiation document and that client activities are shown in the detailed project plan. You, as the Project Manager, must sit down with the client and make sure that they understand and agree the time commitments you are requesting in both the project initiation document and in the detailed plan.

It is important that you agree this with them ahead of time, and that they truly understand the time commitments. You don't want to get into a battle later when things are getting tight on the project and you don't have the time for negotiation. So get an understanding early in the project.

"Gain and maintain the client's commitment. Keep them on board. Make sure they understand how important their time is to the success of the project. It will make your job easier."

Killer Idea 39
Set a tight but achievable schedule on your project.

When I asked the programme manager of one of the biggest programmes in Europe at the time – one that I had the pleasure of working on and a programme that came in on time and within budget – what was one of the things that he thought helped to deliver a successful project, he said, "A tight but achievable schedule."

When there is a tight but achievable schedule, people usually work with a sense of urgency. I believe that people would rather work with a sense of urgency than work in a relaxed laid-back manner. There is a real buzz that a sense of urgency on a project causes – a feeling that we are doing something really important. There is the old saying that if you want to make sure that something gets done, give it to a busy person. The busy person will get it done, whereas the person that is not busy will tend to procrastinate. As Project Manager, we must make sure that we keep our people focused on important activities and then things will get done.

In my experience, I have always attempted to put a plan in place that was tight but achievable. I can safely say that when any of my projects had a tight schedule to meet, my team always seemed to step up to the mark and get it done.

One of the things that you need to watch out for is that the tight but achievable schedule is not too tight and will not, therefore, put too much strain on the team and they are not able to deliver. As the Project Manager, you are the one that needs to control this and I believe that being able to control this comes from experience. Experience in dealing with the client's wants and needs, and an understanding of the team's ability to deliver to those wants and needs. A tight but achievable schedule that is too tight will cause the team to give up and decide that they truly can't deliver to the schedule. So make sure that you hit a happy medium. Not too tight but tight enough.

"Project management becomes very exciting when there is that 'sense-of urgency buzz' surrounding your project. Cultivate it!"

Killer Idea 40
Take massive action but only as defined in the agreed project plan.

ction does not necessarily equal achievement. As you probably know, it is possible to be very active and just be spinning your wheels, staying still. Have you ever spent a day where you were very busy but at the end of the day, you felt that you had not achieved anything of value? I have and I know lots of other people who have done the same thing. So what kind of action equals achievement? The answer is action taken against activities in the project plan. In fact, my suggestion is that you focus on the plan and that you take MASSIVE ACTION against the activities in the plan.

If you have a proper plan in place that the team helped develop and that the project Board approved, then that plan will include all of the products that must be delivered on the project and all of the activities required to deliver the products. In other words, all of the things that need to be done to complete the project are in the project plan. Therefore, the project team should not be spending time working on anything other than the activities in the project plan.

I understand that we sometimes make mistakes and we might miss something that needs to be done. In that case, if there are other things that the Team thinks need to be done, then you must review those things and make a decision as to whether they should be included in the plan or not. If they must be done, then they must be included in the plan. If they are included in the plan, it must be because they are helping to produce a deliverable. If they are not helping to produce a deliverable, then you must ask the question, why do we have to do it?

Let's make sure of four things:

- Our plans are well thought out and we have done everything possible to develop a comprehensive, detailed plan at the beginning.

- Our people have helped us develop the plan and they are in agreement with it.

- Our people understand that they should not work on anything, other than the activities in the plan, without first discussing it with you.

- You decide quickly as to whether the new things should be done or not and, if they are to be done, the plan gets updated to reflect the new activities.

MASSIVE ACTION against the activities in the plan. That's one of the important keys.

"Anybody can take action but it takes really
committed teams to take
MASSIVE ACTION.
Build committed teams and
watch them fly!"

41

Killer Idea 41
Use success words to describe your project; talk about achievement meetings and achievement reports, rather than progress meetings or progress reports.

I think it is extremely important that you, the Project Manager, should set the example when it comes to attitude and behavior. It is important that you continually remind the team "We are here to achieve, to be successful and to enjoy ourselves." Therefore, I feel it is very important that you use "success words" whenever possible. I think that success words help instil a positive feeling on the project – a feeling that we are moving in the right direction.

Also, certain words have a different psychological effect on a person than others. For instance, I know that the word achievement affects me differently than the words progress or update. I never have progress meetings on my projects; nor do I have progress reports. I always have achievement meetings and I always put out achievement reports. I believe that renaming your progress meetings as achievement meetings sets the right tone for the meeting. We are here to achieve and, therefore, I want my team to come to the meeting knowing that they are here to report achievement.

I remember a time when I was on a contract at an investment bank and was asked to look at their Y2K project. The Project Manager was just preparing a report for the Board entitled a programme status report. I told him that I thought he should change it to a programme achievement report. He told me that he didn't think that would be right, as they hadn't really achieved anything since the last report. I asked him if that, in itself, told him anything. In fact, I then reviewed what had been going on since the last report and he was right. They just seemed to be spinning their wheels. I suggested to the Project Manager that he name the report what he was going to name it originally but that we should change it when we next reported. In addition, we should tell the team that we were going to make the change and that we were focusing on future achievement not on update or status.

I suggested that the report should come directly, in an automated fashion, from the plan and then discovered another problem. There was no real plan. Well, there ended up being a lot more to do to bring that project into line than just changing the names of the reports and the meetings, but it was a start. I believe, in line with success words, that when you communicate to anyone about your project, you should be as upbeat and positive as possible.

That doesn't mean lie about how well you are doing if you aren't doing well. What it does mean, though, is be upbeat about what you are doing to fix those things causing you problems. Even when I took on two poorly run projects that were in desperate trouble for the UK Government, I was able to be upbeat in my reports because I was able to discuss the good things that we were doing to bring the projects into line and to turn them around.

Do yourself a favor. Use success words on your projects.

"Instead of using the word problem which presents a negative view of a situation and actually causes you to view the situation negatively, use the word challenge which has a more positive feeling about it."

Killer Idea 42
Be creative in setting up your project control procedures and bureaucratic in following them, rather than bureaucratic in setting up your procedures and creative in following them.

In the past, when I've reviewed IT project control procedures, the one thing that strikes me about them is how bureaucratic they are. And in most cases, I find that the procedures aren't being followed, or the people that are supposed to be following them say that they are following the spirit of the procedures. What they really mean, of course, is that they are not following them and the truth is, that when I review them, I can understand why. I usually find that I would have trouble getting anything done if I did follow them!

What we usually find is that the person or persons who developed the procedures did not have the necessary experience to create them. When the company realizes that they need to have control procedures for their projects to follow, a large majority of them try to develop them on the cheap. That is, they assign someone within the organization to develop them and that person, in most cases, does not have the experience necessary to develop them properly. They might have read a book about the topic that their control procedure is covering, or they may just assume that the task of developing them is just another job that can be done by analysis, design and development. Project

control procedures set up this way are one of the main reasons that they turn out to be bureaucratic.

Project control procedures should be developed by experts in project control. Only experts, people who have done it before, are able to create control procedures that are not bureaucratic, but are creative. Only experts are able to know what parts of the standard control procedures can be given away and which parts of them must be kept – in other words, how they can develop control procedures that are creative yet still deliver the control they are supposed to deliver.

Once the creative control procedures have been developed and agreed, they should be presented to the team for their understanding and they should be followed to the letter of the procedure. Creatively developed procedures should be easy to follow and therefore they do not need to be followed creatively.

They should also be put under change control, so that any change to be made to the procedures must be proposed, its impact assessed, then accepted or rejected by the Project Manager.

"Processes and procedures are absolutely essential to project success. They make up the 20% hard skills in the success equation."

Killer Idea 43
Use the project support office to support the Project Manager and the project team, in the project planning and monitoring process.

Having a really great project planning and monitoring process in place on your project is essential to project success. Yet, a great project planning and monitoring process takes a lot of time and effort. This is where the project support office can truly help the Project Manager and the rest of the project team.

During the planning of the project, rather than have the Project Manager actually input the planning information into the project planning tool, I suggest this activity be delegated to the project support officer. He or she can gather the planning information or, if required by the Project Manager, facilitate the planning sessions with the project team. The project support officer can, once the data is gathered, create the plan and present it to the Project Manager for approval and presentation to the rest of the team. We must remember that, even though the project support officer is preparing the plan from the data gathered from the planning sessions, the Project Manager and the project team still own the project plan. They, in addition to the project support officer, should be committed to the successful delivery of the project in accordance with the Plan.

The Project Manager should also let the project support officer design, develop and implement a project monitoring process. This process should include six important tasks:

- Reporting on achievement by the project team, on a weekly basis, with the project support officer verifying the achievement.

- Updating of the project plan with the achievement data, by the project support officer.

- Chasing by the project support officer of achievement information on activities that should have been reported as achieved but have not been

- Helping the project team to come up with solutions to slipping activities, so as to minimize impact on the project.

- Presenting the updated plan to the Project Manager, along with any challenges and possible ways of meeting them and any other detrimental information applicable to the schedule or to the budget

- Distributing the Project Manager's agreed, updated plan.

This is basically the way that project planning and monitoring support is provided on our projects – and it works.

"A project plan is immensely important to the success of a project but only if it is kept up to date."

44

Killer Idea 44
Use the project support office to provide support to the project manager and the project team, in achievement reporting.

Achievement reporting is one thing that usually takes up a lot of the Project Manager's time and I believe that it shouldn't. In addition, I think that most achievement reports (most Project Managers call them progress reports or highlight reports) are too wordy and do not provide achievement information in an easy-to-understand format. I've also found that as a project gets into trouble, the reports tend to go one of two ways. They either get wordier and wordier or they get fewer and further between with excuses about why they are late.

I think most if not all achievement reports should be prepared by the project support officer. How can this work? Well, the Project Manager should first get agreement with the stakeholders of the project as to what types of reports are required, their contents, their formats and their frequencies. Once this is agreed, the project support officer can then ensure that these reports are prepared as agreed, in order to present them to the Project Manager for his or her approval and for in-time delivery to the applicable stakeholders.

In addition, I believe that the reports should come almost in their entirety directly from the project plan. Reports should show how actual achievement stands up to planned achievement for the period being reported upon. This achievement could cover activities, issues, expenditure, deliverables etc. In all of those cases, besides having planned dates, we should be collecting and reflecting data in the various plans, to show how well we are doing against those planned dates. I know it can be done because I've had it done many time before. I'm not sure how to do it technically, but I know that macros can be written to gather data electronically from a plan to populate a report. The only written words in the reports would be an explanation of any variances between planned and actual achievement. If other areas require drafting, the project support officer can draft those areas, and present the entire report to the Project Manager for approval.

Use the project support office to make you and your team's life easier.

"Achievement reporting is
one of the key ways of
communicating with all of
the stakeholders on
a project."

45

Killer Idea 45
Use the project support office to provide support to the Project Manager and the project team in the change control process.

I have never asked a Project Manager if he or she controls changes and have them say, "No, we just let those suckers fly. We don't really control them." Every Project Manager says, "Yes, we absolutely control changes on our project." However, I have very seldom seen projects where changes were controlled properly. There are a number of reasons for this but I think the main ones are: that the Project Manager doesn't have the time to control the changes as rigorously as he or she should; and, as discussed in Killer Idea 42, that in most cases the change control procedure is written by someone who isn't experienced in change control and so people on the project tend to ignore the procedure or go around it.

I make sure that my project support officer is experienced in change control and I assign him or her to support the project team and myself in setting up and operating a sound process. Change control is not a difficult procedure to put in place but it is sometimes difficult to get people to follow it.

The basic process, as with so many processes, can be shown as a relatively simple step-by-step method. The process must start, however, with agreed documentation. It is once we have agreed a document that changes to the document need to be controlled. The simple process to be supported by the project office, needs four stages:

- The person proposing the change prepares a request for change, or a change proposal, or a change request. The name of the form doesn't really matter but let's call it a change request. The change request is sent to the project support office.

- In the project support office, the change request is logged into the change request database and is distributed to pre-selected reviewers for an assessment of impact on, among other things, the project schedule, cost or technical aspects. The impact assessment is completed and sent back to the project support office

- The project support office compiles all of the assessments into one impact statement and presents the impact statement to the Project Manager and representatives at a change control Board meeting. The chairman of the change control Board discusses the change request with the Board members and then makes a decision as to whether the change request is approved, rejected or deferred.

- The project support office updates the database with the change control Board information and whatever action was agreed at the Board meeting is initiated by those responsible.

Administration of this process takes time and effort that can easily be done by the project support office, leaving the Project Manager with time to manage the project, not having to administer the change control process.

"Project Managers should not be 'bogged down' with administering processes and procedures that could easily be delegated to a less expensive but equally important resource."

Killer Idea 46
Use the project support office to
provide support to the Project Manager
and the project team, in setting up and operating
the project library and reviewing and
approving documents.

ost projects do not have a project library where official copies of documentation are kept. In fact, in most cases, handling of project documentation is done in a rather slipshod fashion. When project documentation is handled properly it is usually because the Project Manager recognizes that it has to be done, rather than the organization having project library standards in place.

I think you should establish your own project library and let your project support office prepare and implement the procedures necessary to run it. This should include processes for storing the project documentation, processes for reviewing and approving documentation, and processes for checking documentation into and out of the library.

On projects that I run, I make sure that all deliverables, once the drafts of the deliverables are completed, are submitted to the project support office, so that they can manage the review process. This process usually includes the distribution of the deliverables to the appropriate people for review, collection of comments and facilitation of the review meeting.

Once the review meeting is conducted and the comments are handled by the deliverable owner, the final deliverable is then checked into the project support office for inclusion in the library. Once the agreed final version is submitted, it is put under change control process and any changes required to be made to the deliverable will have to be done in accordance with both the change control and the document check-out and check-in procedures.

"Effective documentation management and proper change control go hand in hand. You can't have one without the other."

Killer Idea 47
Use the project support office to provide support to the Project Manager and the project team in dependency management.

ost large organizations have loads of projects on the go, delivering all sorts of products, changes and business processes. In addition, there are usually a lot of dependencies among the projects and in most cases, nobody is managing those dependencies and there is no process in place to do so. Management of the dependencies between and among projects has historically been left up to the various Project Managers if it is done at all. I've found this to be wholly unsatisfactory and, therefore, I believe it is important to project success to manage the dependencies from a central organization. I usually assign the responsibility for developing, implementing and operating a dependency management process to the project support office. The project support office is usually in a unique position at the centre of all the projects, or at the very least, independent from the projects and can therefore, have a helicopter view of the dependencies.

The process should include four main steps:

- The initial identification of the dependency.

- An agreement between the Project Manager who must satisfy the dependency and the Project Manager with the dependency.

- Identification of the dependency in both project plans.

- Re-validation of the dependency on a timely basis.

I do not like to go more th an a month for the re-validation of the dependency.

When I was the programme manager for a very large programme with a British bank, I found that managing dependencies among all of the projects on the programme, was a very time-consuming activity. I would not have had time to do it, so if it was going to get done properly, I had to have my project support office do it. And they did a great job.

"The three actions to take with dependencies:

- Minimize as many external dependencies as possible,

- Pull as many external dependencies as possible into your project so that you manage them,

- Track the remainder as closely as possible."

Killer Idea 48
Use the project support office to help administer a risk and issue management process.

Risk and issues management is one of those things that we know we need to do but we don't seem to have the time to do it well. So what do a lot of project managers do? They give lip service to it. They put a risk and issues list together and every now and then they update it but, in between the updates, they really don't have the time to manage the list.

As an aside, another thing I find is that there is usually a big discussion about whether something is a risk or an issue. From a project management standpoint, who cares? Some action is going to have to be taken, whether it is a risk or an issue. You just need to make sure that the action is taken. How do I do it, to make sure that it gets done?

I assign defining, developing, implementing, operating and administering the risk and issues management system to my project support office.

The risk and issues management systems must cater for six sets of actions:

- The initial identification of the project's risks and issues. The best way to do this is in a workshop attended by the applicable stakeholders and facilitated by the project support officer.

- The analysis of each risk and issue. Each risk is analyzed in terms of its impact and the probability of it happening. Each issue is analyzed in terms of its impact on the project if not taken care of and its urgency. I like to use a scale of 1 to 4 in both evaluations with 1 being low and 4 being high. The two numbers are multiplied so that you come out with a single score for each risk and issue. I then pay particular attention to any risks or issues that score 8 or over.

- A discussion and agreement of what actions must be taken to mitigate the risk and handle the issue, and a schedule for when the actions must be taken.

- Monitoring of the actions by the project support office, to ensure that the actions are taken.

- Reporting to the Project Manager and the project team on the risk and issues status for review at each achievement meeting.

- Continued identification, and analysis, of risks and issues during the life of the project.

"Assigning the risk and issues management process to the project support office will be a big help to you and your team. It will save you time and you can be assured that someone is focusing on gathering the information required for management of them."

Killer Idea 49
Think of ways to add value to the weekly achievement meetings held with your management team.

You should be getting your management team together for an achievement meeting on at least a weekly basis. You should also have a standard agenda for this meeting to include:

- Management update.

- Outstanding action items.

- Achievement since last meeting.

- Planned achievement for next week.

- Review of risks and issues.

- New risks and issues.

- Any other business.

However, in addition to items on this agenda, I try to think of ways in which I can add value to the meeting. For instance, one thing that you could do is to ask your team what new technology they might be interested in learning more about and then have a technology expert present the new technology to the team. In fact, you could schedule a whole series of technology briefings to the team. There may be other things that the team are interested in.

You could have senior management or the CEO speak to your team about future plans. Or schedule a briefing from the senior client, explaining how the product or system that the team are delivering fits into the client's overall strategy.

The best way to add the value is to ask the team how you can do that and then take their advice.

"Let your management team know that you are flexible when it comes to the topics covered in the weekly achievement meeting. Ask their advice and then listen to them."

50 Killer Idea 50
Insulate the project team, as much as possible, from the non-project influences, distractions and activities.

I find that there are always loads of non-project demands on my project team. These are the things that every Project Manager, must watch out for. We need to be sure that our people, as much as possible, are insulated from non-project activities. We need to stand firm on this point. Too many times I've seen the time of my people nibbled away by things that senior management would like everyone in the company to do. Things such as surveys to complete, communication sessions to attend, presentations that have nothing to do with my project to give, presentations to attend, training courses to attend, meetings that they are requested to attend, and much else besides. All of these are probably valid things for my people to do but they do eat into their project time – time which they should be spending on the project. I believe that a better time for them to do these things would be when they do not affect the project in an adverse way.

If you are unable to keep members of the team from being called upon to do things that have nothing to do with your project, you should ensure that the project Board is aware of any impact on your project. They may also be able to help you insulate the team.

Remember, the goal is to deliver the project – on time, within budget, to the expectations of the client and to provide a positive experience for your project team. And you and the team must continue to be focused on that goal.

"Non-project demands eat into the project schedule by adding non-project activities to the project team. Do everything you can to keep the non-project demands to an absolute minimum."

51   Killer Idea 51
Appoint a "Minister of Fun" with the responsibility of identifying fun things to do for and with the project team.

I wish that I had come up with the idea of a Minister of Fun but I didn't. The first time I heard of a Minister of Fun being established was by Mayor William Schaefer of Baltimore, Maryland, in the USA. Mayor Schaefer established the role of Minister of Fun with the overall responsibility of coming up with fun things for the people of Baltimore to do – and, if possible, to raise money for the City Treasury while they were doing them.

My favorite fun idea that the Baltimore Minister of Fun came up with met both of the Mayor's criteria. Just before Valentine's Day, the city sold potholes as Valentines. You bought a pothole for $25, or $5 for 'old folks'. The City filled in your pothole, drew a heart with Cupid's arrow through it, put your Valentine's name in the heart, took a picture of it, put it in a Valentine's card, included the address of your pothole and sent it to you to give to your Valentine. A great fun idea and the city fixed their streets.

There was also "Think Pink" Day and other ideas... but you need to read about William Schaefer and his exploits yourself.

But the idea for a Minister of Fun is a good one and one that I have implemented on a number of my projects. Try it on yours and see what happens.

Maybe the Minister of Fun should have a slot at the weekly achievement meeting. Help him or her out by brainstorming fun ideas for the project to do.

Fun things will help to lighten the spirits of the project team and get more done faster.

I've included four ideas below that you may be able to use, or which may help to stimulate your thinking to come up with other ways to have fun at work:

- Sponsor a "show and tell" day where members of the project team bring to the achievement meeting something that they are interested in and would like to share with the team.

- Sponsor a contest to name the project. The best name, chosen by vote of the team, wins a bottle of champagne.

- Have a baby picture day, with all the team bringing in pictures of themselves as babies, and have a contest to see who can match the most pictures with the grown-ups.

- Most people on our projects today seem to be juggling loads of things at work. Well, surprise your team by bringing in a professional juggler, to teach them how to really juggle.

There is a book that I suggest you get. It's called, 301 Ways to Have Fun at Work, by Dave Hemsath. There are some great ideas in the book.

"Life is too short not to be having fun."

And in closing...

Thank you very much for buying this book and hopefully, trying out the Killer Ideas that I have presented to you. Try some of them or all of them and let me know how you do.

On October 23, 2003, I was diagnosed with bladder cancer that had also spread to a number of lymph nodes. After an operation, chemotherapy, radiotherapy, prayer, healing, visualization, meditation and best wishes from friends and loved ones, I was told that I was clear. Now it's just periodic check-ups.

Why do I tell you this? Because at that time, I realized that life is short.

Whenever you start thinking that you have loads of time to become the person you want to be, to do the things you want to do, to have the things you want to have, think again!

During my fight with this disease I realized in my heart, what is truly important in life. Some of the important things are love, family, friends, the spiritual side of life, doing what you want to do, being what you want to be, having what you want to have and, most of all, living life with passion. That was a very loud wake-up call for me. Let's hope that you don't need that type of wake-up call! Just remember...

Life is short! If you are not having fun doing what you are doing then go do something else.

Set goals, work on achieving them – but always, and I mean always, enjoy the journey!

God bless you and keep smiling!

Richard's Professional Biography

Richard has been called the 'Red Adair' of the project management world. In case you don't know, Red Adair was the larger-than-life oilfield firefighter, who people called when they had a major oilfield fire. Richard is the larger-than-life Project Manager who they call when they have a major problem with their projects. Richard is an American who has been living in England since 1981. He is a very experienced Project Manager, project troubleshooter and professional speaker. His experience ranges from the dizzy heights of putting a man on the moon as part of the Apollo Programme team, to working as part of the management team that computerized the British income tax system, to leading the delivery of two major systems for the 43 police forces in England and Wales. He has directed major programmes of work for some of the largest companies in the world.

Richard is the founder, chief executive and leader of Pulse 8 Limited and the founder of Inspiration Systems Group. He now devotes most of his time to running Pulse 8, senior-level consulting, lecturing, teaching his Morreale Master Classes and speaking engagements.

With over 30 years of management experience, Richard is able to consult and speak with authority. He speaks on many different facets of management and personal development topics. His speeches and presentations can be specifically tailored for your organization and your conference.

Richard is a member of the National Speakers Association in the United States and the Professional Speakers Association in the United Kingdom. He is a highly motivated, enthusiastic and energetic individual who knows how to motivate his people to exhibit the same traits.

Richard's varied background and experiences have made him a highly sought after project troubleshooter, Project Manager and professional speaker. His background also provides him with fertile ground for his speeches and presentations. If you show up for one of Richard's talks, you will, judging from feedback received so far in his career, enjoy listening to him. One thing is for sure – he will enjoy presenting it.

"Wherever you go -
There you are!"

Richard's Personal Biography

ichard and his wife Linda have 7 children between them (6 of his and 1 of hers), 9 grandchildren and 2 great-grandchildren. Richard wants you to know that he is not as old as this might suggest because he started very early in life. With all these people running around, you could be forgiven if you were to mistake one of Richard's former occupations to be that of a producer. He has (not necessarily in the order given):

- Worked as a door-to-door salesman selling encyclopedias to families.

- Worked as a door-to-door salesman selling cookware to single working girls.

- Worked as a door-to-door salesman selling shoes to anybody.

- Worked as a stock clerk in the Winn Dixie Super Market, in Bay St. Louis, Mississippi.

- Spray painted enamel sidings for petrol stations.

- Worked in construction.

- Played guitar in a rock and roll band.

- Been a deck-hand on a shrimp boat.

- Managed a number of rock and roll bands.

- Been a docker on the waterfront in New Orleans.

- Collected bad debts for a loan company.

- Worked on a land survey team.

- Been a butcher in a grocery store.

- Worked as a bartender.

- Worked as an Organizer for the International Brotherhood of Electrical Workers (for one day) picketing an electrical plant in the deepest part of backwoods Mississippi (he lasted until the police were called and his boss was asked where his permit allowing him to picket was, and the boss said it was the First Amendment to the US Constitution which, by the way, was not the right answer as it landed the all of them in jail for the night).

- Worked in a number of increasingly important roles on the Apollo Space Programme.

- Worked as a consultant with the National Oceanic and Atmospheric Administration.

And all of this before he was 30. By this time, he had also fathered 6 children (where did he find the time?).

While working with the US Government as a Project Manager in Washington DC, he and his ex-wife (yes, he's had two) lived on a farm in the Blue Ridge Mountains of Virginia where they raised animals, vegetables and children (not necessarily in that order) as part of a back-to-the-country self sufficiency kick. It wasn't as successful as it could have been, because no one in the family really wanted to eat the pigs or chickens, and since most of the family wanted to read rather than weed, the vegetable crop didn't set any records either. It was then that he decided to move to California where, besides working full time, Richard completed a 4-year university degree in Business in 24 months.

He then went back to work in Washington DC and was subsequently asked by his employer to transfer to their European division to work on the British income tax system project - the computerization of PAYE. He was later made to a director of the UK company but after 18 months, he realized that he wasn't having fun any more, resigned and started his own consultancy company.

Richard's varied background and experiences have made him a highly sought after project troubleshooter, Project Manager and professional speaker. His background also provides him with fertile ground for his speeches and presentations. If you show up for one of Richard's talks you will, judging from feedback received so far in his career, enjoy listening to him. One thing is for sure – he will enjoy presenting it.

Richard Morreale & Associates
8 Atlantic Square
Station Road
Witham, Essex. CM8 2TL
United Kingdom
www.RichardMorreale.com
richard@RichardMorreale.com

Managing Smaller Projects: A Practical Approach

So called "small projects" can have potentially alarming consequences if they go wrong, but their control is often left to chance. The solution is to adapt tried and tested project management techniques.

This book provides a low overhead, highly practical way of looking after small projects. It covers all the essential skills: from project start-up, to managing risk, quality and change, through to controlling the project with a simple control system. It cuts through the jargon of project management and provides a framework that is as useful to those lacking formal training, as it is to those who are skilled project managers and want to control smaller projects without the burden of bureaucracy.

Read this best-selling book from the U.K., now making its North American debut. IEE Engineering Management praises the book, noting that "Simply put, this book is about helping people control smaller projects in a logical and effective way, and making the process run smoothly, and is indeed a success in achieving that goal."

Available in print format. Order from your local bookseller, Amazon.com, or directly from the publisher at

www.mmpubs.com/msp

The must-have book for "accidental project managers"— those who have PM roles suddenly thrust upon them.

It's late Friday afternoon and you have just been told by your boss that you will be the project manager for a new software development project starting first thing on Monday morning. Congratulations! Now, if only you had taken some project management training...

This book was written as a crash course for people with no project management background but who still are expected to manage a small software development project. It cuts through the jargon and gives you the basics: practical advice on where to start, what you should focus on, and where you can cut some corners.

This book could help save your project... and your job!

ISBN: 1-895186-75-7   (paperback)

Also available in ebook formats. Order from your local bookseller, Amazon.com, or directly from the publisher at **http://www.mmpubs.com/surprise**

Managing Agile Projects

Are you being asked to manage a project with unclear requirements, high levels of change, or a team using Extreme Programming or other Agile Methods?

If you are a project manager or team leader who is interested in learning the secrets of successfully controlling and delivering agile projects, then this is the book for you.

From learning how agile projects are different from traditional projects, to detailed guidance on a number of agile management techniques and how to introduce them onto your own projects, this book has the insider secrets from some of the industry experts – the visionaries who developed the agile methodologies in the first place.

ISBN: 1-895186-11-0 (paperback)
ISBN: 1-895186-12-9 (PDF ebook)

http://www.agilesecrets.com

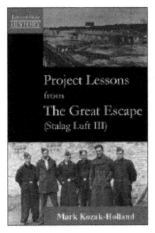

Project Lessons from The Great Escape (Stalag Luft III)

While you might think your project plan is perfect, would you bet your life on it?

In World War II, a group of 220 captured airmen did just that – they staked the lives of everyone in the camp on the success of a project to secretly build a series of tunnels out of a prison camp their captors thought was escape proof.

The prisoners formally structured their work as a project, using the project organization techniques of the day. This book analyzes their efforts using modern project management methods and the nine knowledge areas of the Guide to the *Project Management Body of Knowledge* (PMBoK).

Learn from the successes and mistakes of a project where people really put their lives on the line.

ISBN: 1-895186-80-3   (paperback)

Also available in ebook formats.

http://www.mmpubs.com/escape

◄ The Project Management Audio Library ►

Negotiation Basics for Project Managers

By Mark Miller

www.PM-Audiobooks.com

Do you always get what your project needs when you negotiate?

Negotiation skills are critical for success in project management. The project manager depends on top management, other functional managers and the project team members for the resources and support needed to complete the project. Project managers negotiate the scope of the project, the budget, timeline, resources and changes that arise during the project.

A manager with good negotiation skills can reach a win-win agreement and still achieve better results than an unskilled negotiator. This audio CD provides project managers with a crash course on negotiating and includes the objectives for negotiations, the traits needed to be a successful negotiator, the various steps that negotiations go through, tactics you can employ to improve your chances of success, and common negotiation mistakes.

ISBN: 1-897326-63-7   (audio CD)

Order from your Amazon.com or directly from the publisher at **http://www.PM-Audiobooks.com**

Your Future as a Project Manager

A question that is continuously being asked by project managers in every industry is "What demands will executive management expect from me and what skills will I need to maintain my value within the organization?" This is a question that addresses the future state of the project management profession and emphasizes the need to consider the rapid changes we are all experiencing. The future is, in most cases, unpredictable but the project manager can prepare and plan for changes as the business environment continues to evolve. This planning includes the identification of key competencies and a process for continued professional development.

This recording focuses on the current trends impacting the professional project manager and provides some key strategies and steps that a project manager can take to achieve success as World Class Project Manager.

ISBN: 1-895186-39-0   (Audio CD)

http://www.PM-Audiobooks.com

 **The Project Management Audio Library**

In a recent CEO survey, the leaders of today's largest corporations identified project management as the top skillset for tomorrow's leaders. In fact, many organizations place their top performers in project management roles to groom them for senior management positions. Project managers represent some of the busiest people around. They are the ones responsible for planning, executing, and controlling most major new business activities.

Expanding upon the successful *Project Management Essentials Library* series of print and electronic books, Multi-Media Publications has launched a new imprint called the *Project Management Audio Library*. Under this new imprint, MMP is publishing audiobooks and recorded seminars focused on professionals who manage individual projects, portfolios of projects, and strategic programmes. The series covers topics including agile project management, risk management, project closeout, interpersonal skills, and other related project management knowledge areas.

This is not going to be just the "same old stuff" on the critical path method, earned value, and resource levelling; rather, the series will have the latest tips and techniques from those who are at the cutting edge of project management research and real-world application.

www.PM-Audiobooks.com

www.ingramcontent.com/pod-product-compliance
Lightning Source LLC
Chambersburg PA
CBHW071134050326
40690CB00008B/1464